FOR LEAH

IF DUCKS CARRIED GUNS

AND OTHER IFABILITIES

BY MICK STEVENS

A FIRESIDE BOOK

PUBLISHED BY SIMON & SCHUSTER INC.
NEW YORK • LONDON • TORONTO • SYDNEY • TOKYO

Fireside
Simon & Schuster Building
Rockefeller Center
1230 Avenue of the Americas
New York, New York 10020

FIRESIDE and colophon are registered trademarks
of Simon & Schuster Inc.

Manufactured in the United States of America

10 9 8 7 6 5 4 3 2 1

Library of Congress Cataloging in Publication Data

ISBN 0-671-65997-9

IF ROME **HAD** BEEN BUILT IN A DAY

IF WHEN A TREE FELL IN THE FOREST EVERYBODY HEARD IT

IF GUILT WAS DISPOSABLE

IF NOBODY WAS CUTE

IF IGUANA WAS THE FLAVOR OF THE MONTH

REAM ◆ ICE CREAM

IF STEPHEN KING WROTE COOKBOOKS

IF EVEREST WAS JUST A PROP

IF BEES WERE HOUSE PETS

IF SPAGHETTI WAS ALIVE

IF CHUCK BERRY PLAYED THE TUBA

IF GASOLINE WAS FREE

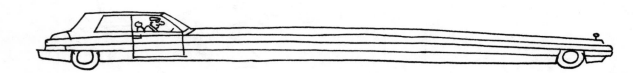

IF A THOUSAND PICTURES WERE WORTH ONE WORD

IF BAD BACKS WERE GOOD LUCK

29

IF THERE WAS DESIGNER FRUIT

IF DOGS WERE IN CHARGE

IF LETTUCE WAS FATTENING

45

49

IF OKRA WAS AN APHRODISIAC

IF PEOPLE LIKED COCKROACHES

IF JELLO WAS GOLD

IF THERE WAS NO TV

IF YOU COULD LEAD A HORSE TO WATER, MAKE IT DRINK, AND FORCE IT TO SING "THE STAR-SPANGLED BANNER"
OH, SAY CAN YOU SEEEEE...

IF TEXAS WAS TROMPE L'OEIL

HOWDY PARTNER! WELCOME TO TEXAS!

IF VACATIONS CAME IN BOXES

IF ROLLS-ROYCE MADE VACUUM CLEANERS

IF MOUNTAINS WERE MOLEHILLS

IF MOTHERS HAD THEIR OWN TV SHOWS

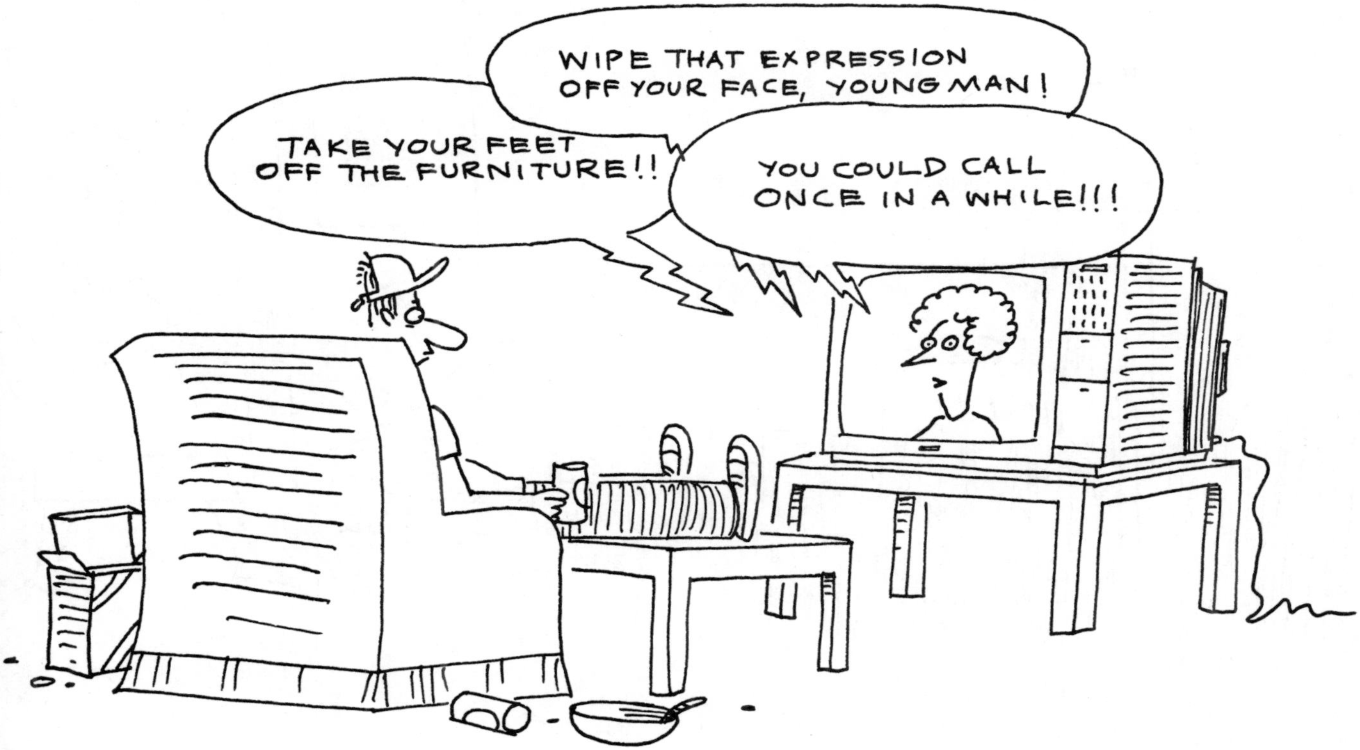

IF CARPETS GREW

IF IT TOOK AN APPLE, SIX TOMATOES, 27 EGGPLANTS, A BANANA, AND ELEVEN WATERMELONS A DAY TO KEEP THE DOCTOR AWAY

IF YOU COULD GROW YOUR OWN FURNITURE

IF THERE WAS **EVERYTHING**-FREE COLA

IF MONOPOLY WAS A SPECTATOR SPORT

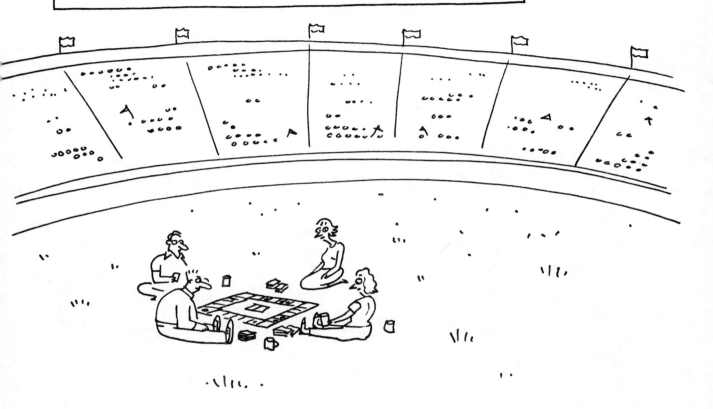

IF BANK ROBBERY WAS LEGAL

IF SNACKING WAS ILLEGAL

IF SOFAS WERE SACRED

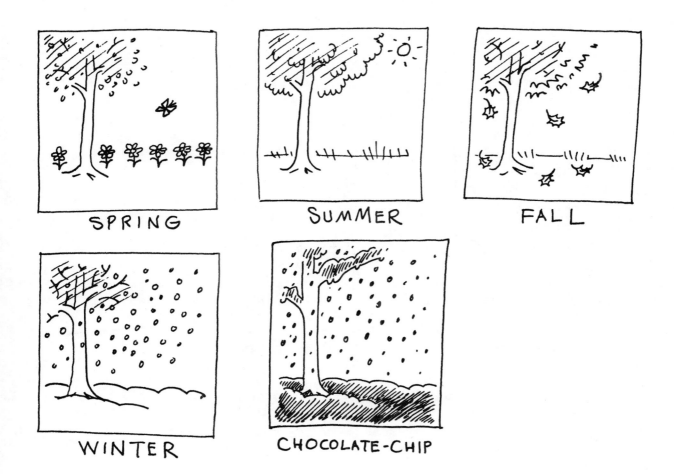

IF THERE WERE FIVE SEASONS

SPRING

SUMMER

FALL

WINTER

CHOCOLATE-CHIP

IF MOODS COULD BE REPAIRED

IF ONE-EYED LITHUANIAN COMPUTER PROGRAMMERS WITH ODD HAIRCUTS AND LOUD TIES MADE BETTER LOVERS

94

96

IF GRAVITY TOOK THE DAY OFF

IF YOU COULD GET YOUR BRAIN WASHED

Speedee
BRAIN
WASH

102

IF "PARMESAN" WAS A DIRTY WORD

112

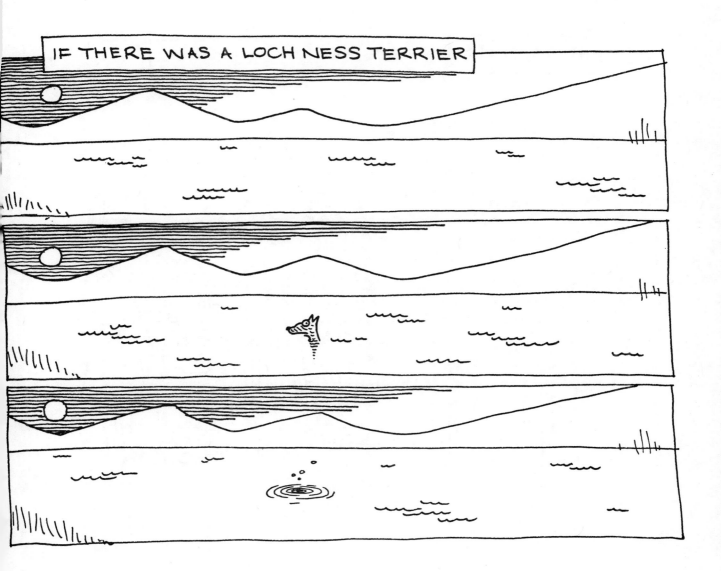

IF THERE WAS DIET TV

IF AIRPLANES HAD BALCONIES

IF THERE WERE STUNT FLIES

123

IF YOU COULD BUY A 30-PIECE SUIT

IF LIFE HAD REMOTE CONTROL

MORE

LESS

BETTER